DEDICATION

This Book Is Dedicated To All Who Desire To Be Financially Free. May Your Efforts Bear Fruits In the Near Future And I Wish You All The Success In Life.

&

I dedicate this book as well to my two beautiful children and my loving wife who have been nothing short of being my light and joy throughout the years.

Copyright 2017 by Jonathan S. Walker - All rights reserved.

The following eBook is reproduced below with the goal of providing information that is as accurate and reliable as possible. Regardless, purchasing this eBook can be seen as consent to the fact that both the publisher and the author of this book are in no way experts on the topics discussed within and that any recommendations or suggestions that are made herein are for entertainment purposes only. Professionals should be consulted as needed prior to undertaking any of the action endorsed herein.

This declaration is deemed fair and valid by both the American Bar Association and the Committee of Publishers Association and is legally binding throughout the United States.

Furthermore, the transmission, duplication or reproduction of any of the following work including specific information will be considered an illegal act irrespective of if it is done electronically or in print. This extends to creating a secondary or tertiary copy of the work or a recorded copy and is only allowed with express written consent from the Publisher. All additional right reserved.

The information in the following pages is broadly considered to be a truthful and accurate account of facts and as such any inattention, use or misuse of the information in question by the reader will render any resulting actions solely under their purview. There are no scenarios in which the publisher or the original author of this work can be in any fashion deemed liable for any hardship or damages that may befall them after undertaking information described herein.

Additionally, the information in the following pages is intended only for informational purposes and should thus be thought of as universal. As befitting its nature, it is presented without assurance regarding its prolonged validity or interim quality. Trademarks that are mentioned are done without written consent and can in no way be considered an endorsement from the trademark holder.

CONTENTS

PART 1

Introduction

Chapter 1: Why Your Attitude Matters

Chapter 2: The Steps To Writing A Non-fiction Book

Chapter 3: Edit, and then Edit Some more

Chapter 4: Formatting Your Book in the Best Way

Chapter 5: Distributing Your Book To Attract Readers

Chapter 6: Advertising Your Book the Right Way

Part 2

Chapter 1: Do You Have Traction?
Chapter 2: Offline
Chapter 3: Emails

Chapter 4: Viral
Chapter 5: Public Speaking

Part 3

Chapter 1: Establishing Your Own At-Home Product for Sale

Chapter 2: What Shopify is and How to Use It

Chapter 3: The Basics of Dropshipping

Chapter 4: How to Maximize Your Profits with Amazon FBA

Conclusion

VIP Subscriber List

Dear Reader, If you would like to receive latest tips and tricks on internet marketing, exclusive strategies, upcoming books & promotions, and more, do subscribe to my mailing list in the link below! I will be giving away a free book that you can download right away as well after you subscribe to show my appreciation!

Here's the link: http://bit.do/jonathanswalker

Introduction

Congratulations on purchasing your personal copy of *Book Launch Success Formula: Your Ultimate Guide to Write, Publish, Market, and Launch Your Non-Fiction Book to the Best Sellers List*. Thank you for doing so.

The following chapters are going to explore how you can write, publish and promote your own non-fiction book for profit. If you've always dreamed of creating a work of non-fiction that is full of educational, inspirational, or interesting content, then know that there is no reason why this dream can't become a reality. After reading this book, you will have all of the tools that you need in order to write a non-fiction book that is attainable from the reader's perspective. There are many aspects of a book that you need to consider that take place before, during and after the writing process is completed. This book is going to prompt you to think about all of these factors so that there's no chance you'll end up forgetting about any important aspect of the non-fiction book writing process. If you follow the steps that are presented in this book, there's no doubt that you'll be an established author in no time.

There are plenty of other books on the market regarding this topic. Thanks again for choosing this book!

Chapter 1: Why Your Attitude

Matters

Before we get into the specific details regarding how to write a successful non-fiction book, it's important that you understand the mindset that you should be cultivating as you move towards developing your first book. If you don't go down this path with some sort of plan, it's likely that success will be more difficult to achieve. Having an understanding of your own personal goals and mindset throughout the writing process will allow you to see your book with more objectivity. This will hopefully lead to more efficiency and productivity throughout the entire book-writing process.

Knowing What You Want

People seek out sources of passive income for a variety of reasons. For some, writing a book in the hope of achieving passive income is all about the bottom line. For others, the book writing process is more about self-discovery. There are also people out there who are simply looking to convey information to a larger audience. These types of people might be thinking very little about how much money they're going to make or what their potential for income can be through writing non-fiction books. Whatever your individual aspirations are when it comes to writing your book, it's important that you take some time to figure out what these reasons are.

If you can, try to dissuade yourself from writing your book "because you want to." Yes, writing a book out of simply a desire to do so is perfectly fine; however, when you begin to think about what is truly motivating you to write a non-fiction book, you'll be able to make decisions about your book based on this recognized motivation. In other words, when you're able to focus in on your motivation, you'll be able to work towards something tangible, rather than working towards an unclear or changing ideal.

Don't Allow Yourself to Get in Your Own Way

Writing a book is not for the faint of heart. Sure, these days it can be argued that the internet has made it easier than ever before to be able to distribute a non-fiction book, but this does not mean that your book is necessarily guaranteed to be a success. For this reason, aspiring authors of all types have been known to get in their own way when it comes to being able to achieve their writing goals. If you're serious about writing not just a non-fiction book but any type of book, you can't allow your brain to go to a place where it's telling you that you won't be able to achieve your goals. Some common setbacks that authors can think about and sometimes believe once they say it enough include the following statements:

"I'm not good enough as a writer, no one is going to read my work."

"There are so many better writers out there who already have written about this same topic. How am I supposed to compete in this competitive market seriously?"

"These techniques have worked for other writers, but they are not going to work for me because _____ (fill in the blank)."

You may already have started to hear these types of whispers in your head. If you have, then it's important that you pay them no mind. Steady yourself against these types of thoughts, and be sure to create a mechanism for yourself that will allow you to ignore any negative thoughts that may enter your head during the entire writing process.

Tackle this Book One Goal at a Time

The next chapter will discuss multiple steps involved when you're attempting to write a book. It's important to tackle the writing of a book in small chunks, rather than become flustered as you attempt to take on too many elements of the book at once. Once you have an idea of what it is you're going to be writing about, you can then move towards breaking the book writing process into step-by-step pieces. It might be a good idea to create small weekly goals for yourself, as this will allow you to stay on track and focused on one task at a time.

Chapter 2: The Steps to Writing a Non-Fiction Book

Once you've established the proper mindset in your head, you will then be ready to tackle the steps that are necessary for the writing process. This chapter is going to look at what these steps are so that you can make sure that you're covering all of your bases when it comes to writing your first non-fiction book. Remember, taking these steps one at a time will help you to feel in control and on top of the writing process as a whole. You're also going to find that writing a non-fiction book, in particular, takes considerably more work than does a book that is of another genre.

Step 1 to Writing a Non-Fiction Book: Understand What You're Getting Into

One of the first aspects of writing a non-fiction book involves understanding the genre in which you're going to be writing. Even within the non-fiction genre, it can be argued that there are sub-genres that you need to consider if you're thinking about writing that type of book. Some of these sub-genres include memoirs, biographies, or even history. In addition to considering the various types of sub-genres that exist, you also need to keep in mind that non-fiction literature is all about facts. Unlike fiction, you cannot simply write down whatever you think might be true about a given topic. Instead, you need to make sure that your book is full of information that is *correct*. If you don't fact-check your work, it's more than likely that your book will be considered poorly written.

Step 2 to Writing a Non-Fiction Book: Read Up

If you're having trouble figuring out exactly how you want to write your non-fiction book, you should consider reading some non-fiction books in your spare time. A few renowned non-fiction authors include Erik Larson, Tom Wolfe, and A.J. Liebling. When you read a well-written non-fiction book, you should be paying closer attention to how the book is written, instead of attempting to retain all of the information in the book. In any industry, trying to learn from the best is never a bad idea.

Step 3 to Writing a Non-Fiction Book: Choose Your Topic

Perhaps you already know what you're going to write about, or maybe you're in a position where you need to narrow down your list of potential topics and focus on just one.

When you're figuring out your topic, you should be trying to be as detailed as possible. If you have too many points of interest in a single book, the result could end up being sloppy. Additionally, you should also be thinking about how you can write something that will have a unique perspective or will shed light on something in an innovative way. Lastly, when you're choosing your topic, you should also be considering your audience. Who is going to be reading this book, and will this audience be large enough to attract adequate attention? No one wants to write a book that isn't going to be read. If you personally enjoy a subject matter but don't think that there is a lot of interest beyond yourself, it might be best to reconsider your topic.

Step 4 to Writing a Non-Fiction Book:

Conceptualize Your Book

Once you have a general topic, you then need to start narrowing in on what it is you're going to say and how you're going to say it. Some questions to consider include the following:

- What will the tone of your book be? How will you ensure that this tone will remain consistent throughout the whole book?
- What angle will your book take?
- How will your book be outlined? Why are you going to choose to outline it in this way?
- Brainstorming can also be beneficial during this step in the non-fiction book writing process. Don't be afraid to document ideas that you're not even going to end up using. Try to get as many ideas that you can down on paper because it's likely that one of these ideas will be the one that makes

you say, "Aha!"

- Step 5 to Writing a Non-Fiction Book: Research
    - Once you've concretely decided on the topic about which you're going to write, the next step is to start doing your research. One of the first questions that you should ask yourself in regards to this step involves how much research needs to be done? Some great research techniques include interviewing first account witnesses to events, finding experts on the subject of your choice, and doing research at libraries. In addition to figuring out how you're going to conduct research, you should also be setting up a research checklist for

yourself. This will ensure that you don't forget to look into something that is crucial to what you're going to be writing.

-

- **Step 6 to Writing a Non-Fiction Book: Write the Book**

    - After you have taken the time to do your research and have made sure that your research checklist is complete, you will finally be ready to start writing your book. Similar to the research phase of your book, before you start to write you will want to outline a writing schedule for yourself. The best way to organize your schedule is to either go by page or word count. Also, keep in mind that you might be more "off" than "on" when it comes to writing quality content. The best piece of advice here is to be strict with yourself when it comes to meeting your deadlines, but also create your schedule in a way that provides you with some leeway for unforeseen circumstances.

Chapter 3: Edit, and then Edit Some More

Obviously, after you've finished writing your book once, you are far from being finished with it. Sure, you may have initially been in the mindset that you simply wanted to get your words down on a page, but after your first draft, it's time to get serious about the quality of the writing that you've done. This chapter is going to discuss how you can edit your non-fiction book properly, without any outside help. Yes, you may want another set of eyes on your book before publishing it, but this does not mean that you can't edit your book yourself as well. It should be mentioned that editing is an incredibly important aspect of the writing process. Being lazy with editing will likely result in a book that is good, rather than great.

-
- **Editing Tip 1: Read Aloud**
-   Your book is going to sound different aloud than it does in your head. Additionally, reading your book aloud will force you to slow down and truly see the words that you've written. Doing this will not only enable you to find grammatical errors or typos in your work; it will also allow you to find any sentences or phrases that may seem awkward or out of place.

-
- **Editing Tip 2: Trim the Fat**
-   Another great tip for when you're editing your book is to go through it

and eliminate any excessive words that you've used. These days, people have an even shorter attention span than ever before. For this reason, you do not want your book to be bogged down with words that make your sentences long or your point difficult to grasp. It's best to keep your sentences short.

- Editing Tip 3: Read Your Book from Multiple Perspectives

- Another way that you can go about finding anything that needs to be edited is to read the book through different methods. For example, if you have typed most of your book on the computer, print it out and read it in a hard copy version. If you have been printing out your book and reading it away from your computer, try reading your book when it's on a screen. Finding a new perspective is sometimes all it takes to realize that you have a lot of editing to do.

-
- Editing Tip 4: Get Grammatical on Yourself
- When you're writing your book, you want to make sure that most of the verbs that you're using are active, rather than passive. Passive voice is used when describing something that has already happened, while the active voice is used when you're describing something that is taking place in the here and now. Even though you're likely going to be writing about something that has already taken

place, you should use the active voice while writing a book. The active voice keeps the reader engaged, and makes the information seem current and relevant while it's being read. Go through your book and circle any words that are passive in nature. Then, replace them with active words.

Editing Tip 5: Don't Sound So Serious

If you've ever read a book where the author comes off sounding a bit pretentious, then it's likely that this author used too many big words while writing his or her book. No one wants to read a book that needs a dictionary to go along with it. Especially if you're writing a non-fiction book for the first time, it's best to use an informal tone when writing your book. This will allow you to dictate your points properly and will ensure that you're using all of the words in your book correctly.

-

- **Editing Tip 6: Avoid the Word "I"**
-   When you're writing non-fiction, you want the book to focus on the events that you're documenting, rather than yourself. This is an important point to make, especially when you're looking to be informal yet informative. Yes, using the word "I" in your work is certainly informal, but it is largely considered to be a bit too informal in the non-fiction literary world. If you have the urge to use the word I, take some time to think about how you can reconfigure your sentence in a way that doesn't use that

word. While it may seem difficult at first, avoiding the word I is a habit you should try to learn as an aspiring non-fiction writer.

- Editing Tip 7: Describe, Don't Narrate

Even though you're writing a non-fiction book, this does not mean that your book should not be descriptive. Think about it this way; you don't want your book to feel as if the person reading is reading a cookbook. Instead of telling the person who is reading the book what happened in a dry or underwhelming fashion, try to create a story for the reader to some capacity. Yes, a non-fiction book should be factual, but it can be intriguing to the reader at the same time. Keep this in mind as you edit your book. If you come across sections of your book that are guilty of being a bit too narrative, see if you can play around with editing this section in a way that will speak to your readers in a more descriptive manner.

- The editing techniques that were presented in this chapter should be considered even as you write the first draft of your book. The more editing tips that you can keep in mind while you write, the less editing you will end up doing once your first draft is finished. Remember, your book is constantly going to be a work in progress. If you find a lot of problems in the first draft of your book, it's important to not become discouraged with yourself. We all make mistakes. It's more important to handle these mistakes with efficiency than to become mad at yourself when you miss the mark of perfection.

- **Chapter 4: Formatting Your Book in the Best Way**

- When you're finally happy with how your book reads and feels from the perspective of your audience, the next step is to work towards getting it published. Of course, publishing companies and people who format books for a living are probably not going to want to be handed a book that is unorganized. Instead, there is a general formatting standard that these companies expect when they receive a book from a potential author. This chapter will go over how you can format your book in a way that will end up saving you both time and money when it's time to find yourself a publisher. It's also important to note that the formatting guidelines could change depending on the publisher that you're using. In addition to following the tips presented in this chapter, you should also check with the publisher that you end up using to see what their formatting guidelines are.

-
- Formatting Technique 1: Formatting Your Title Page

- The publisher will not care about what your cover page or back page looks like initially. You typically will not need to send these pages to a publisher. Instead, the first page of your book should be your title page. On the title page, the title of your book should be in the middle of the page. Underneath of the title, you should include your name (the author's name), along with your book's word count, and your contact details. This way, the publisher will be able to contact you easily.

-

- **Formatting Technique 2: Set Your Page Parameters Correctly**

- Generally speaking, a publisher is going to expect you to have the margins of your book set to 3 centimeters on all sides of the page. They will also be expecting that the alignment of the document is set to the left-hand side. The document should be double-spaced. Lastly, you should format the indents of your book through the formatting options on your word document. To do this, go to Format, then Paragraph, and then Section. From here, set your indents up to be 1.25 centimeters. This will ensure that all of your indentations are uniform.

-

- Formatting Technique 3: Stick to Italics

- For non-fiction books, in particular, italics are always used. You never want to underline a word in a non-fiction book. There is no real reasoning behind this; it's just a rule that all non-fiction writers follow.

-

- **Formatting Technique 4: Avoid PDFs**
- When you know that you're going to be sending your document off to a publisher for review, you don't want to convert your Word document into a PDF file. Doing this will likely change the formatting of your document, which will create errors in your document when the publisher changes the document back into a Word file.

-

- **Formatting Technique 5: Each Chapter Should Be a New Page**
- Instead of having each chapter following the previous one, you should use the page break function within Word in order to break up each chapter onto a new page. Additionally, some people think it's a good idea to save each chapter of their book as a new file. This is not a good idea. If you do this, the publisher is likely to send the book back to you for further editing.
-
- **The Cost of Publishing a Book**

- Now that you're aware of the primary formatting standards that exist within the publishing industry, you may be wondering about how much it costs to get a book published. This cost is largely going to depend on whether you choose to publish the book yourself or go through the formal publishing process. If you're planning to use the formal publishing process, the cost of the book could be between $500 to $700. If you choose to publish the book yourself, it is likely going to cost you between $200 to $300. There are pros and cons to each route that you can consider. Let's take a look at some of these advantages and disadvantages now.

-

- **Getting Published is Validation**

- As you're going to find, writing a book can be a rather stressful process. While you may think that the book that you're writing is good, how do you know whether or not the book is going to be received in the way that you hope? When people go through a traditional publisher, they are typically rejected a few times prior to signing and deal and getting a contract. Once the contract is signed, this can be an incredibly great feeling for a writer who had doubts that he or she could actually do it. On the other hand, if you don't really care about whether or not your book is "good" from the perspective of the publishers, then you may opt to self-publish your non-fiction book.

- **Working with a Publisher Guarantees a Team Effort**
- When you work with a publisher, this company is going to make sure that your book is edited to perfection. They are also going to make sure that the cover of your book looks professional, and that your book is advertised properly. If you think that you can handle all of the responsibilities that come with being your own publisher, then self-publishing will save you money; however, when you work with a publisher, you are able to truly see a professional book deal at work.

Chapter 5: Distributing Your Book to Attract Readers

As you saw in the previous chapter, there are both advantages and disadvantages that exist when you're deciding on whether you want to publish your book yourself or whether you want to have a professional publishing firm do it for you. Instead of harping on the pros and cons of each avenue, this chapter is going to focus on how you can distribute your book through both methods of publication. This way, regardless of whether or not you plan to self-publish your book, you will still be able to benefit from this chapter.

How to Get Your Book into Retail

Stores

Obviously, you are probably hoping that your non-fiction book is going to lead to some income. The only way to achieve this goal is to distribute your book to as many people as you possibly can. If you decide to use a publishing firm to complete your book, then they will be able to distribute your book for you. That's part of their job, and they're good at it. One of the ways that they're able to easily distribute books is through slashing the book's price significantly. In fact, most publishing companies offer books to retail stores for as much as 50% off the asking retail value of the book. The hope is that by significantly discounting the price of the books, more retailers will be more enticed to purchase the books in bulk.

- Even though the publisher already has these connections available, this does not mean that it's impossible to get your book into a retail store on your own. It might take a bit more work on your end in order to achieve this, but it's certainly doable. Below are some tips that you can use if you've decided that you're interested in taking the route of self-publishing.

1. Highlight that You're a Local Author: While you may not be able to get the attention of a global retail store from the onset, you can instead opt to go to an individual retail store in your area and pitch your book to them. By highlighting the fact that you're a local author, you might be able to generate some appeal for your book that would otherwise not be there.

2. Look for Similar Titles in the Store: Prior to speaking with anyone at a major bookstore or retail

store such as Target or Walmart, it would also be a good idea to go to the book section of the store and see what they're carrying that relates to what you've written. Once you know what they carry, you can should then speak to someone about possibly adding to the collection that they already have. Doing this will make you look as if you've done some groundwork.

3. Make Sure Your Book Cover Looks Fresh: While your book's cover should look professional regardless of whether or not you're self-publishing it if you're going to be attempting to distribute your book on your own, this concept is doubly important. Retailers are going to be much less likely to hear you out if the cover of your book looks amateur. Perhaps having a professional design your book's cover, even if you're going to be self-publishing it, would be the best move here.

4.

5. Understanding Commission Costs

6. While you might be thinking that it would be worth it to get yourself a publisher who can distribute your

book for you, it's important to understand how commission works in the publishing world. If you go through a publishing company, they are going to be making a pretty penny off of the work that you've done. On average, the royalties that you'll receive on a book when you use a publisher can be between seven to twenty-five percent. When you compare this to a self-published book, self-publishing a book might be the preferred way to go.

7. For example, if you decide to self-publish a book and put it on a digital platform such as Kindle or Nook, you are going to be receiving around seventy-percent in royalties. Of course, if you self-publish a book and attempt to sell it to a retail store, they

are going to expect to receive a large discount from the retail price. These are all important factors that you need to consider, regardless of the publication route that you take. If you decide to self-publish, it's advised that you offer a retail store around a fifty-five percent discount on your book. This way, it's more likely that they will agree to keep it in their store for you.

8.
9. Host a Book Signing or a Launch Party
10. Lastly, another way that you can attempt to distribute your book to the fullest extent possible is through a launch party. This event will highlight the release of your book and will allow you to advocate for the purchase of your book. If you already have your

own website or blog site, this would be a great place to advertise this type of party. If you don't have your own site, social media sites such as Facebook or Instagram are two other platforms where inviting people to your launch party might be appropriate. This is a fun and lighthearted way to generate awareness about your book, without directly having to ask people to buy it.

11. Chapter 6: Advertising Your Book the Right Way

12. It's important to understand that distributing a book and advertising a book are not the same thing. This makes sense. Once you have distributed your book, you want to advertise it so that it will receive as much attention (and money) as

possible! This chapter is going to go over how you can advertise that your book is for sale, with special emphasis on the fact that the internet is a great way to promote a book on the cheap.

13.

14. Book Advertising Idea 1: Make a Trailer for Your Book

15. A fabulous way to advertise your book is to make some type of trailer for it that can be uploaded to the internet. Once you create this video, you can then easily and cheaply upload this video to multiple social media sites. Some apps that you can check out if you're interested in making a book trailer include Animoto, Prezi, or PhotoShow.

16.

17. **Book Advertising Idea 2: Create a Photo Sweepstakes**

18. If you have a large social media following already, a photo sweepstake is a great way to generate awareness and excitement around the book that you've written. To do this, simply create an advertisement of some kind stating that you are hosting a photo sweepstakes. Make sure that the prize for the sweepstakes is good enough for people to want to participate. The flyer should also state the rules for the sweepstakes. Simply instruct people to send in a picture of themselves holding a copy of your book, and the funniest picture that you receive will win the sweepstakes prize.

19.

20. Book Advertising Idea 3: Advertise at a School

21. We all have probably attended an assembly at school at some point in our lives. If you have connections with teachers or anyone who works at a school, you can try to set up an assembly for the students about the information that can be found in your book. When you get in front of a large crowd, the hope is that these people will be able to talk about the buzz of your book to others, and possibly attract more people to the sale of your book.

22.

23. Book Advertising Idea 4: Advertise on Facebook

24. Posting an advertisement on

Facebook is fairly simple to do and does not have to cost a lot of money. For example, one option that you have when you want to advertise through Facebook is to pay sixty-five cents per click. This means that every time your advertisement entices someone to click on your ad, you pay Facebook sixty-five cents. This is just one example of the types of advertising options. There are many different types of ads that you can choose from on Facebook. The most important factor to consider when you're seeking to advertise on Facebook is the time in which you decide to buy ad space. For a book, you're going to be better off scheduling your ad around a holiday. This way, people might want to buy it as a gift for a loved one.

25.

26. **Book Advertising Idea 5: Put a Link to Your Book in Your Email Signature**

27. When you put a link to your book in your email signature, you are able to reach out to people with whom you're corresponding without directly saying to them, "Hey, I wrote a non-fiction book. Buy it!" Doing this will undoubtedly attract people to your book, yet you won't have to make anything awkward.

28.

29. **Book Advertising Idea 6: Create a Brand Around What You've Written**

30. Let's pretend that you wrote a book on the effects of childhood obesity on future generations. Your research

has revealed the negative implications of obesity in the world, and your book is advocating for the elimination of fast food worldwide (a bold claim, yes). Instead of simply writing your book and waiting for the sales to start, a much smarter technique would be to create a brand around the topic of your book. Create a website, gain a following. This will allow you to not simply gain an audience; it will help you to gain the trust of people who are interested in the same things that you are.

31. In this way, you have the potential to become an advocate and an expert on the non-fiction topic of your choosing, all without having to get a degree. Along these same lines, you can also use your own backstory as a

way to generate interest around your book. Do you suffer from the same things that your book is about, such as anxiety or a particular illness? If you can personally relate to the topic about which you choose to write, that's all the more reason to create a brand around yourself that will showcase the bring awareness to the topic. This will make you seem more relatable from an advertising and promotional perspective.

32.

33.

34.
35.
36.
37.

38.
39.
40.

41.

42. PART 2

43.

44.

45.

46.

47.

48.

49.

50. DO YOU HAVE TRACTION?

51. New startup companies and businesses will often have a hard time getting up and running. Being able to get the capital to fund a new business and keep it going can be hard for new businesses that don't have the time to prove their abilities in the marketplace. When a business creates traction, it helps the company to attract possible investors and gain an edge over their competition.

52. Business traction tells us the progress a new business has and its momentum it gains as it grows. There isn't a certain way that a company can measure traction, but most businesses rely on their revenue and how customers respond to their product. The reason for traction is to make sure the business grows and meets certain objectives and goals. This may seem like an abstract thought, it is imperative and allows a business to understand where, in the industry, it stands and where they want to get.

53. Traction may be important to the company's founders and workers; it is also equally important to stakeholders and investors who are interested in the

organization. The better the traction, the more investors that company will attract. As a result of attracting more investors, the company will also have more funds available to them to help them succeed. This means that developing good business traction is imperative to all new businesses and should be a part of the company's business plan.

54. The first steps to creating a successful startup are, understanding the organization's future, creating goals, and figuring out a way to reach those goals. Having clearly stated goals in your mission statement and your business plan will show investors how they can expect the company to progress in relation to the factors of the marketplace and competition. However, just coming up with your goals isn't enough. To know your traction, you have to understand the metrics you will be using to define your success. Depending on what industry you're in and the external factors of the marketplace, traction could be measured through market research, sales, or customer response.

55. Even the most well-intentioned company, with a perfect business plan, can still struggle to find traction. There are millions of reasons as to why so many startups fail, the most common is a lack of

brand or product awareness. When competition begins to grow in the marketplace, the smaller businesses that aren't as well known will become overwhelmed by larger brands. To avoid this problem, new companies need to increase the marketing and advertising efforts.

56.

57.

58.

59. OFFLINE

60. When online marketing started to grow in popularity, people forgot about the many proven offline marketing methods. Online marketing is important, many of the other techniques in this book are online, but engaging your customer's offline is a distinct and unique method that shouldn't be forgotten.

61. If you're looking to boost your marketing, start trying some outside of the box tactics. Let's look at five almost forgotten offline marketing methods that require little to no budget.

62. OFFLINE GUERRILLA MARKETING

63. Guerrilla marketing refers to the use of unique marketing methods, and since online marketing is so strictly structured, offline is the easiest area to try out some guerrilla marketing tactics. At this point, you can forget everything you know about how marketing channels work and allow your inner child to have some fun. Offline guerrilla methods include:

- Create temporary images on cars, buildings, etc. with sticky notes.

- Create branded bookmarks and give them to your local library.
- "Accidentally" leave behind a pen with your brand on it at the bank.
- Draw advertisements on the sidewalk with chalk.
- Place sticky notes with your business on it in random places.
- **BUSINESS CARDS**
- This is a guerrilla tactic that needs to be talked about specifically. This is a necessity and not an option like the other methods I mentioned earlier. If you run a business of any kind, whether established, small, or a startup, you have to have business cards, and you need to hand them out. Don't just give them to people that you meet; drop them everywhere you go.
- Places you should leave behind a business card at:
- Always drop your business card in a contest fish bowl that is asking for cards.
- Place your business cards in books at the library that relates to your company.
- Whenever you see a public bulletin board; pin your business card to it.

- When you pay your bill at a restaurant, leave behind a business card.

- **PHOTOGRAPH AND FILM EVERYTHING**

- Since social media marketing is only online, most marketers and owners will forget that they can boost the social campaigns through offline efforts. Simple ways to do so is by taking photos of daily activities and company events and post them online. You can do the same with videos as well. If you or somebody else from your company speaks at an important event, record the speech and upload it to your social media accounts.

- When you use real-life photos and videos from your company's offline world, you are showing your company's personality and increasing your user engagement. A Facebook post that has a photo will receive 84% more clicks, and two times as many like than a text-only post. There are also a lot of social media networks that are the only image based, such as Tumblr, Pinterest, and Instagram.

- **DONATE PRODUCTS AND GIFT CERTIFICATES AS A PRIZE**

- When you offer your service or product as a prize for a local contest, you will build your business's visibility, while also showing that you are committed to your local community. If your business is a beauty supply store, you could donate a gift certificate or a gift basket for your most popular products. The organization you donate the product or service to may even announce your brand prize to a room of sponsors. They may even publish you business names in ads in various publications, like a press release, website, or newsletter.

- **MAKE PUBLIC APPEARANCES**

- Public events provide you a great way to build your brand's awareness, meet new people, and share ideas. They become even more effective when you speak at these events. Locate a local event that is related to your industry, figure out what people want to learn about your business, and volunteer to speak. If you don't have the clout to get to speak at these sorts of events, just attending them can be as worthwhile.

- You don't have to use all of these offline marketing methods, just start implementing at least one. Write down a promotion on a few sticky notes and take them with you. You never know what could happen.

-

-
-
-
-

- **E-MAILS**

- Your average consumer's inbox is full of marketing messages with attention-grabbing subject lines trying to compete with you. Each day there are over 144 billion emails sent out; making email marketing one of the best online channels for business marketing and communication. The trick is to separate yourself from everybody else.

- Figuring out your key message is important to your bottom line no matter what your goal is. The following eight email strategies will ensure that your emails will stand out amongst your competitions, and will help you achieve your goals.

- **PERSONALIZE WITHOUT THE CONSUMER'S NAME**

- You know longer have to worry about "Dear [insert name here]." Having a personalized email greeting isn't as effective as you may think. Research performed by Temple's Fox School of Business has even suggested that this personalization can be harmful. People become wary about emails with personalizing greetings because of the concerns about credit card fraud, phishing, and identity theft.

- An important part of email marketing is the relationship. Does your recipient trust you? Does the recipient actually know who you are? When you send out an email the jumps the familiarity gun too soon, your personalization will appear to be a bit sketchy. Intimacy had to be earned in the real world, so emails work the same way.
- When you fake familiarity, you will likely turn many of your email readers off. Now, this doesn't mean that all personalization forms are off limits. In fact, certain brand personalizations can help you out: sending an email that gives your subscriber individuality. This could simply mean their purchase history.
- This means if you want to personalize your emails, do it in a meaningful way. It doesn't take much of relationship or knowledge to put your consumer's name in your email greeting. Sending a personalized email that is recipient specific shows a lot more care.
- THE IMPORTANCE OF SUBJECT LINES
- It seems that when it comes down to crafting your subject line, there is only one thing you have to avoid: a 60 to 70 character subject line. Marketers call this the subject length "dead zone." Research

performed by Adestra tracked over 900 million emails, and there wasn't any increase in click-through or open rates at the 60 to 70 character subject line length.

- On the opposite side of things, subject lines that contained more than 70 characters were more beneficial in engaging readers and getting them to click through to the content and subject lines that at less than 49 characters tested better for email open rates. Surprisingly, they found that subject lines that had less than ten characters at 58% open rate.

- The use of short subjects came into vogue when President Barack Obama used them in his fundraising emails. There was amazing engagement with subject lines such as "Wow" and "Hey."

- Now the question is: Are you looking for opens or boost clicks? Create long subject lines for more click-through, or keep them short for more opens. Either way, just make sure that you keep your subject lines out of the 60 to 70 character range.

- **EMAIL PRIMETIME: 8 PM TO MIDNIGHT**

- While quality emails may be created during regular business hours, the ones that are more likely to be open aren't sent between nine and five. The best time to send an email is at night. Experian Marketing Services discovered that the emails that received the best open rate had been sent between 8 pm and midnight. This time not only did well for open rates, but it did better for sales and click-through. 8 pm to midnight is also the least used, which helps the late night emails perform better than the rest.

- Deployment time and inbox crowding also work together. This means that if your email goes out at a time when others don't, it stands a better chance of being noticed. Mailing your customers at their optimal time will be up to you. You will need to make sure at run some tests to see when you receive the best response.

- **EVERYBODY LIKES SOMETHING FOR FREE**

- Consumers love receiving things for free. Bluewire Media tested different types of content on their 6,300 subscribers to find out what free items got the highest clicks and open. Their winners were tools and templates.

- Most consumers will want to know what's in it for them and Bluewire Media found that tools and templates greatly outweighed photo albums, brain teasers, expert interviews, and ebooks. You will have to do your own tests with your own subscribers, but using this information is a great head start.

- **OPENS ON MOBILE DEVICES ACCOUNTED FOR 47% OF ALL OPENS**

- Look at it this way, if your emails get you $100,000 in sales every month, would you want to say goodbye to $44,000 just because you emails show up weird on mobile devices?

- You need to make sure you design you email responsively so that they look great no matter where they are being read. These are some mobile design tips that can help:

- Ergonomic: Most people with scroll and tap with their thumb, so place interactive elements in the middle.

- Make an obvious, and easy to use, call-to-action. Above the fold it best.

- Make sure you follow the iOS guidelines for buttons: 44 pixels wide by 44 pixels tall.

- Make your font size better to make them easier to read on smartphones.

- Change your email to a one column template.

- **EMAIL IS BETTER THAN TWITTER AND FACEBOOK**
- **Social media may be on email's heels, but the inbox kind still has a greater influence over social media. SocialTwist monitored 119 referral campaigns for over 18 months that were performed by leading companies and brands. They found that there was a significant advantage to an email's ability to create new customers as compared to Twitter and Facebook. There were 300,000 referrals that became new customers, and of that 50.8 % were reached by email, 22 % through Facebook, and 26.8% through Twitter.**
- **EMAIL ON WEEKENDS**
- **Saturday and Sunday didn't outperform the 8 pm to midnight time, but they did outperform the other weekdays. Just like at the 8 to midnight time, a number of emails sent on the weekends are low, which helps your messages to stand out. The margins for sales rates, click-through, and opens were not that substantial, but every little bit counts when it comes to email marketing.**
- **RE-ENGAGING OLD SUBSCRIBERS**
- **You have a huge list, awesome. The problem is that 2/3s of those people are likely inactive. Research has**

discovered that a subscribers list of inactivity is 63%. This means that once a person joins your list, they are less likely to actually follow up with any of your emails. Listrak has said that the first 90 days are important to change a sign-up to a devotee.

- That 63% now needs to be re-engaged. The trick is to figure out what kind of re-engagement campaign will work the best for you followers. It's quite likely, that if you have already been doing research, you have found different kinds of results.

- **VIRAL**

    - It's true; the term viral marketing does sound offensive. Saying that you are a viral marketer will likely cause people to take a couple of steps back. A virus is a feared thing, which is not quite dead and not completely alive. But you have to admit a virus is admirable. It is able to live in secrecy until it is able to reproduce several times. It even piggybacks onto other hosts to increase its own tribe.

    - So how does a virus translate to marketing? Viral marketing is a strategy that gets a consumer to pass on a message to other people, which create a potentially exponential growth in the influence and exposure to the message. Like a virus, these strategies take advantage of fast multiplication to send out a message to thousands or even millions.

- Hotmail.com is a classic example of viral marketing at work. Their strategy was simple:

1. Give people free email addresses and services
2. They placed a tag at the bottom of each message that said: "Get your private, free email at www.hotmail.com."
3. Then they sat back and waited while people emailed their family and friends
4. People notice the emails
5. Those people register so that they get their own email; all leading up to
6. They pass the word on to a growing number of associates and friends.
7. Their message spread like the small waves that ripple off of the water after a pebble is dropped into a pond. You too can make a viral marketing strategy that ripples out to more and more people.
8. Before you begin coming up with your strategy you have to accept the fact that some strategies will work better than other ones depending on your audience. There is very few that work as well as the

Hotmail message. But we are going to look at six unique concepts that you should try to use in your marketing plans. Your strategy doesn't have to contain every single one of these elements, but the more that you use, the more powerful your result will become. An effective strategy should try to have:

1. Service or product giveaway
2. Makes it easy to transfer to others
3. Is able to be scaled from small to large
4. Taps into common behaviors and motivations
5. Makes use of existing networks for communication
6. Use others' resources
7. Let's look at each of these a little more.
8. SERVICE OR PRODUCT GIVEAWAY
9. Free, like we've talked about before, is a powerful word in marketing. Most of the viral marketing programs out there will give away valuable services and products to attract their consumer's attention. These free things could be free "cool" buttons, free information, free email services, or free software programs that are able to do powerful things, but not everything that the "pro" version is able to do. The words inexpensive and cheap will generate some

interest, but the word free will do the same only faster. Viral marketers aren't afraid of delayed gratification. They are okay with not make any profit today, but if they are able to create a bunch of interest from free things, they will be able to profit soon and for forever. You have to have patience. Free will attract eyeballs, those eyeballs will then wander to the countless things that *aren't* free which you're selling, and there you have sales. Eyeballs will provide you with sales opportunities, email addresses, and advertising revenue.

10. MAKES IT EASY TO TRANSFER TO OTHERS

11. Doctors and nurses will tell you that during flu season, you should do everything in your power to avoid being contaminated. This is because viruses are only able to spread when they can be easily transmitted. The medium that you use to carry your marketing message needs to be easily transferred and replicated: software download, graphic, website, and email. Viral marketing works amazingly on the internet since there are inexpensive and easy communication sources. Digital formats make it easy to copy things. When you look at it in terms of marketing, the entire idea is to make things as simple and shareable as possible. Generally, when it

comes to a marketing message, short is the way to go. Make sure that your message is copied, compelling, and compressed at the bottom of each of your email messages.

12. IS ABLE TO BE SCALED FROM SMALL TO LARGE

13. However you decide to transmit your message, the ultimate goal should be that it's super simple for it to catch fire and spread. To look back at the free email accounts method, there's a fundamental flaw: if the campaign is *too* effective, more users may end up trying to join than server space is available. Otherwise, the new users will be left unaccommodated, and as a result, the campaign will start to fail. Nobody wants a worthless email account, even if it is free. Taking it back to the virus analogy, if the virus is to kill the person that is hosting it before the virus is able to transmit itself, the virus effectively is failing at its job. However, if the email provider were to plan ahead so that the new accounts could certainly be properly be accommodated, regardless of how successful the campaign is, then everything will be alright. The key point is that everything has to be scalable in terms of your campaign; if it can't go from small to big with no problems, then there's a fundamental flaw.

14. TAPS INTO COMMON BEHAVIORS AND MOTIVATIONS

15. A good marketing campaign will always tap into humanity's seedy mental underbelly. Greed drives people. People want desperately to be "cool", as well as loved and understood. By taking advantage of these perfectly human tendencies, you'll generate hundreds of thousands of website hits and millions of email mentions. So, in order to build a strong marketing plan, you have to take advantage of our most human qualities and desires; that, friend, is how you build a winning marketing plan.

16. MAKES US OF EXISTING NETWORKS FOR COMMUNICATION

17. Most everyone is social. Social scientists have figured out that everybody has at least 12 people in their network of associates, family, and friends. Their broader network might consist of thousands of people; ultimately this depends upon what they do and how important they are. For example, a waiter may talk with a huge number of customers every week. The best marketers are those who have a strong understanding of how powerful these interpersonal bridges can be, whether they are strong interpersonal bridges - like those with family

and friends – or weak ones, like with customers. Everybody who uses the internet also has a rather extensive network, as well. They get favorite websites and email addresses. Affiliate marketing programs take advantage of these internet-based networks. The way to rapidly make your message spread is to find your way into these interpersonal connections.

18. USE OTHERS' RESOURCES

19. The best marketing strategies are those that take advantage of others' resources to help get the word out. Affiliate marketing plans, for example, put graphic links or text on other people's websites. A single news article, if pertinent and popular, will be taken up by a huge number of other websites and sources of content. Somebody else's web page or newsprint is relying on your marketing message. Somebody else's resources get depleted and not yours.

20.

21.
22.
23.
24.
25.

26.

PUBLIC SPEAKING

One of the many responsibilities of being a small business owner is being the face of your company. You are already the main customer relationship manager. You must be its lead promoter and champion to grow your business. One way that this can be done is to actively participate and attend conferences that are related to your industry. Another way is to give talks to potential customers.

The following resources and tips can help you find speaking opportunities and conferences that are relevant to your business. They can also help you get speaking engagements, too.

Learning to listen before you speak is an excellent idea. Before you begin doing your own presentations you need to attend sessions that others in your fields are giving. You will pick up on what presentations are popular. You might see gaps that you might be able to fill with your own expertise. If you ask questions and provide different insights during the question and answer time during these presentations, you might be remembered if you apply to speak at a related event at a later date.

33. When you feel like you are ready to represent your business and share your expertise, you will need to find speaking engagements. You need to find groups that are looking for speakers and sell yourself on your talk. The first thing to do is to make a speaker's one-sheet. This is a one-page introduction to your topic and yourself. It will provide a jumping-off point for self-promoting yourself as a speaker.

34. Now you need to look for organizations that are looking for speakers for certain events. You can do a google search to look for speaking events in your area. There are also paid services that will match speakers with certain event organizers. You can offer your services to groups that may benefit from your expertise.

35. To be a successful speaker you have to provide some value to your audience. This means that you have to share your expertise not just promote your business. Your first presentation will be the hardest. You will get better with time. You will start getting reviews and testimonials that you will be able to use to help promote yourself as a speaker. You will soon find yourself being regarded as an expert and the face of your company and industry.

36. Here are some ways to get speaking engagements to help market your business:

1. Become a better speaker: This sounds obvious, but by being a more polished, engaging speaker, you will gain more opportunities to speak. If you are a very good speaker, you can ask for testimonials from the people that invited you to speak. These testimonials go a long way when others are looking for speakers.

2. How can you become a better speaker? The best and easiest way is to record each presentation and watch it later. Take notes of what you would like to improve on. Try focusing on different things every time you speak. How you stand, where you put your hands, how you modulate your voice. With time, you will be an extraordinary speaker.

3. Know your material: Knowing your material inside and out will help you become a better speaker because it will ease your nerves. First, you absolutely must know your speech. You need to practice it over and over. By knowing your speech means you can be confident and at ease when you step on a stage and face the crowd. Being prepared is a great way to overcome nerves.

4. Knowing your speech isn't enough. You must be an

expert in your area. The more that you know, the more confident you will be when taking questions from your audience.

5. The most important thing about your presentation it that it is not a pitch. You should not be trying to sell anything. Give the audience things they can take with them that they can use and actions they can follow. Your main goal is to help them.

6. Have a speaking page on your website: Add a page that promotes yourself as a speaker. It is the best way to get engagements. On this speaking page, post a demo reel, maybe a few clips from a previous engagement that you have posted on YouTube. Include a biography, topics that you can talk about, and titles of some signature speeches you can give in a moment's notice.

7. A page that shows your availability and expertise as a speaker allows event planners and others to see you speak and get a feel of what you will be like on stage. They like to see that you can actually engage with an audience.

8. Build the right relationships: Many business owners think they must speak at large corporations or events to market their businesses effectively. This is

not true. There are plenty of small groups that want to hear what you have to say. The most important thing is to have a clear target market and speak where they are going to be.

9. When you find some businesses, ask them what topics they want to hear about. Give them your one sheet and tell them that you are available to speak. If you have an engagement that is open to the public, send an email to contacts and invite them to come. If you add a video to your website, send a link with a not about the topic and video.

10. Someone you have been building a relationship with will have an opportunity for you to speak. You have been persistent, and they will think about you first.

11. Speak for free: When you first start to speak, you should do it for free. This could mean you might have to speak free for years before you ever get your first paying gig.

12. Speaking for free gives you the expertise to be good enough to not charge for your speaking services but to speak at larger venues.

13. When you can start charging to speak, you will have good reasons to continue to speak for free. When you know that you will not be traveling for a while, send out

emails to local contacts and let them know that you are in town and have time to speak.

14. For local gigs, offer a lower rate or do them for free especially if it is a group within your target market. You just might walk away with some new business.

   15.
   16.
   17.
   18.
   19.
   20.

21.
22.
23.

24.

25. PART

3

26.

27.

28.

29. Chapter 1: Establishing Your Own At-Home Product for Sale

30. Before you begin using any of the online forums that are going to be discussed, it's important that you first establish the type of product that you're going to sell. If you already have a product that you're selling online, then you've completed this step, but you may also be in a situation where you don't know what you're interested in selling at all. Let's take a look at some considerations you need to be making so that you can use Shopify, dropshipping, and Amazon FBA to the fullest extent possible.

31. You Need a Product

32. It's important to understand that in order to use the three online revenue techniques that are going to be discussed later, you need a physical product to sell. Selling a service, or selling something that is

made digitally will not allow you to use the three platforms that are going to be discussed in this book. This does not mean that you need to create this product from scratch yourself. Instead, you can opt to re-sell a product that you get for a discount and then can charge your customer full price. You can also adapt a product that is already on the market. Below are a few considerations to make while you're figuring out what it is you'd be interested in selling for profit:

33. Keyword Research

34. SEO stands for Search Engine Optimization, and SEO research has become one of the primary ways that aspiring online entrepreneurs figure out what is in high demand on the internet. Keyword research involves understanding what people are typing into their Google search bar the most often and then cater your website to fits needs that already exist. If you're interested in doing some keyword research of your own, some of the best SEO websites include the following:

- Google Keyword Planner

- SEMrush

- SpyFU

- Serpstat

    - Unfortunately, keyword research is a marketing tool that is currently in high demand. For this reason, a good keyword search tool is not going to be free. In fact, these tools can cost you upwards of $20 per month; however, if you're serious about getting an online business going, it's worth it. Keep in mind, when you're doing keyword research, you want to find keywords that are high in search volume but low in competition. Most of these SEO tools will provide you with a percentage of how competitive the keywords that you're searching are.

- Notice a Trend as Early as Possible

    - You don't want to be targeting a niche that already has a lot of competition within it. For example, if you wanted to sell yoga mats online, you are going to be competing against major corporations like Lululemon. Your product is likely to drown against competition that has millions of dollars behind it. If you can, you should begin to think about and notice trends that could be up and coming. Then, target those as soon as you can. Social media and other internet avenues can help you to figure out what these trends are.

    -

Chapter 2: What Shopify Is and How to Use It

Once you've figured out what it is you're going to sell, you can then work towards figuring out how you're going to set up your online presence and brand. A great way to accomplish these types of goals is through a service known as Shopify. Shopify can be best described as a platform that makes creating an online store as easy as possible. Let's go through the steps that you'll need to take in order to set up an online shop through Shopify.

Step 1: Sign Up

The first thing to do when you're looking to open an online shop with Shopify is to sign up on their website. Simply head to www.shopify.com, provide them with your email address and click on the large blue button that says, "Get started." Remember, you're going to want to provide Shopify with the email address you want to use for your online shop, rather than your personal email address. From here, Shopify will also ask you the name of your business.

- Step 2: How Will You Use Shopify?
- After you've provided Shopify with your basic information, it will then ask you whether you plan on using Shopify as an online store, or as a tool that you will be using inside of a physical store where you rent or buy space. Finally, it will also ask you questions that have to do with the types of taxes your store will be paying. These questions include ones related to where in the country your store is located or where you will be conducting your business from when you're online. They will also ask you whether you're already selling product and what your annual revenue is expected to be.
- Step 3: Add Your Products
- Next, add your products to your store's page. You will need to upload pictures of what you're selling, along with descriptions of the item, and the item's cost.
- Step 4: Make Your Store Your Own
- Once you've uploaded the products to your online store, the last step involves heading to Shopify's dashboard. From here, click on the tab that's labeled, "Customize the Look of Your Site." This tab

allows you to change features of the store's layout itself and will also allow you to truly make your online store your own. Changing these features does not require programming knowledge, which will make customizing your site a breeze.

- Shopify's Domain Platform
-   Shopify allows you to either add a domain name from scratch or transfer a domain that you already own to your online Shopify profile. Within your dashboard, click on the tab that's labeled "Add a Domain." From here, you will be provided with the option to register a new one or add one that's already been purchased. If you are purchasing a new one from Shopify, this will cost you around $9.00 for the year. As you can see, Shopify makes it easy to both purchase a new domain or transfer one.
- How to Get Paid
-   Finally, the last aspect of Shopify that is crucial to turn on is the payment processor. Again, head to the dashboard and click on Payments. From here, you can choose from many different payment processors. Shopify also has its own payment processor. Once you've chosen the type of processor you'd like to use, be sure to click on "Launch Website." Please keep in mind that if you're transferring a domain, you may

need to wait a few days before the domain that you're transferring has been linked to your online Shopify store.

-
-
-
-
-
-
-
-
-
-

Chapter 3: The Basics of Dropshipping

If you're not interested in setting up your own online store and are instead looking for a less formal way to make money via the internet, then dropshipping may be just the route you want to take. This chapter will discuss the ins and outs of dropshipping so that you can maximize your revenue with this particular method.

The Logistics of an Online Business

One aspect of the online store that Shopify does not account for is shipping. If you're serious about developing an online method of profit for yourself, then the way in which you're going to ship your products to your customers is an important consideration that you need to be making. When you're thinking about this, there are a few factors that you need to take into account. These include how to keep your shipping costs as low as possible, and where you are going to store your product inventory. If the product that you're selling is small, then storage will likely not be an issue for you; however, if you're planning to sell products that are bulkier, then storage space is something that you'll likely need to have. This where dropshipping can come in handy.

- **Shipping to Your Customer from a Vendor's Website**
-     If you're not planning to actually create a product yourself to sell, then you can instead simply advertise goods on a website and then ship them directly to your customers from the vendor's website. To do this, all you would have to do is create a price for the product on your website that will allow you to still make a profit after accounting for shipping costs. You will also probably need to spend money on advertising your products, to ensure that people will buy them. It's important to note that you're likely going to get more bang for your buck this way if you choose to promote products that are on the expensive side. This way, your profit margin will likely be greater than if you choose to sell products that are cheaper.
- **How to Negotiate with a Dropshipping Service**
-     While purchasing a product and choosing to ship it directly to a customer can be perfect for someone who is simply going to be re-selling a product, if you are creating something that you've made to sell online, then you may not be able to simply ship a

product from a vendor's site. Instead, you will have to negotiate with a dropshipping service. This will require some legwork. First, you'll have to reach out to find a drop shipper who will be willing to discuss doing business with you. You'll also have to figure out whether or not this company would be willing to store your products for you in their warehouse. Lastly, you may want to find out whether or not this distributor would be willing to put your logo or company's name on their packing slip when they ship your product for you. This will make your product seem more professional, even though it is being shipped from an auxiliary source.

- These days, there are plenty of websites that have already worked through the process of negotiating with a dropshipping service on your behalf. Some of these websites include WholeSale Central, Alibaba, and Oberlo. For all of these sites, you can find products that fit the theme of your website and can be drop shipped from a manufacturer. Not only will using these types of websites save you time; they will also allow you to cut down on the cost of resources such as tape or boxes. These shipping costs can add up, which is why dropshipping can be a lucrative tool to use when you're looking to operate a simple, yet effective, online business.

-
-
-
-
-
-

Chapter 4: How to Maximize Your Profits with Amazon FBA

- The FBA in Amazon FBA is short for Fulfillment by Amazon. If you've ever wondered how Amazon can reach such a large audience of people and seems to have any type of product you can ever imagine, the answer in part has to do with Amazon's FBA program. This service essentially allows you, the seller, to host your products on Amazon's website. This means that if you decide that your website is going to sell running shoes, then you can post the products that you're selling to Amazon's website. If someone sees your running shoe product and wants to purchase it, they are able to do so through the Amazon platform. This allows you to reach a wider range of people than would otherwise be possible if you were simply selling on your own smaller Shopify website. Let's take a look at how Amazon FBA works in more detail.
- How to Become Involved with Amazon FBA

- Becoming a seller through Amazon has never been easier. Simply head to amazon and create an account for yourself. After you've opened up a seller account through Amazon, you will then be prompted to start uploading your products to your seller portal. Once your products have been placed on Amazon's website, you will then need to ship your products to an Amazon shipping center. You can print out a shipping label from your Amazon FBA portal. This shipping center will essentially be the place where your products will be stored until someone buys them. Once purchased, Amazon will handle the process of shipping your product to its customer. It's also important to understand that you are still able to sell the products that you send to Amazon from other online platforms. If you end up selling your product to a customer on Etsy for example, Amazon will honor this sale and ship the product back to you. This provides you with the added flexibility of being able to sell your products on multiple platforms simultaneously.

- The Cost of Amazon FBA

- Amazon FBA is not free. In fact, it will cost you a little over forty dollars per month if you want to start using this service. In addition to forty dollars, Amazon will also charge a fulfillment fee for each product that you sell. This means that they are taking a cut of whatever you're selling for themselves. For example, if you were to sell a $50 pair of running shoes through Amazon and charge a $10 shipping fee, you are going to end up with $51 after the sale has been completed. This means that if you originally bought the shoes for $50, you're only going to be making a $1 profit. This is why it's important to understand your profit margins for each product prior to selling them on Amazon. Lastly, it's also important to keep in mind that Amazon is going to discount your shipping rates to them once you subscribe to Amazon FBA. Additionally, many items that are sold through the Amazon FBA program and offered to customers with a free shipping option. This feature will undoubtedly entice your customers to purchase.

-

-

-

- Conclusion

- Thank you for making it to the end of this book, *Book Launch Success Formula: Your Ultimate Guide to Write, Publish, Market, and Launch Your Non-Fiction Book to the Best Sellers List*. Hopefully, this book has been able to get your wheels turning and has excited you about not just writing your first non-fiction book, but also how to edit it, promote it, and distribute it properly. All of the information that was presented in this book is crucial when you're attempting to write not just any non-fiction book, but a great non-fiction book. With this book as a handy guide, success if much more likely.

- Your next step is to get to planning! Remember, when you're writing a non-fiction book the planning and research process is arguably more important than the actual content that you end up producing. If the information that you're presenting in your book is false or fluff, your audience is going to know! Do yourself a favor and do the work ahead of time to make sure that the content that you're producing is factual, interesting, and will lead people to feel excited when they open your book. Non-fiction books do not have to be boring. The truth can be just as exciting as a piece of fiction.

- **Again, thank you for taking the time to read this book! Now get out there and write your own great piece of non-fiction!**

- THANK YOU

-

- Dear treasured reader, I would like to thank you from the bottom of my heart for choosing to purchase this book. I hope you've gotten some valuable information that you can use right now to build a successful online business for yourself. If you liked it, would you be so kind as to leave an honest/positive review for my book on amazon. I would appreciate it very much.

In case you missed it earlier, if you would like to receive latest tips and tricks on internet marketing, exclusive strategies, upcoming books & <u>promotions</u>, and more, do subscribe to my mailing list in the link below! I will be giving away a free book that you can download *right away* as well after you subscribe to show my appreciation!

Here's the link: <u>http://bit.do/jonathanswalker</u>

-

Once again thank you and all the best to your success!
Jonathan S. Walker

- About The Author

Hi there it's Jonathan Walker here, I want to share a little bit about myself so that we can get to know each other on a deeper level. I grew up in California, USA, and have lived there for the better part of my life. Being exposed to many different people and opportunities when I was young, it made me want to strive to become an entrepreneur to escape the rat race path that most of my peers had taken. I knew I wanted to be able to travel and experience the world the way it was meant to be seen and I've done just that. I've travelled to most places around the world and I'm enjoying every minute of it for sure. In my free time I love to play tennis and believe it or not, compose songs. I wish you all the best again in your endeavours, and may your dreams, whatever they may be, come true abundantly in the near future.

www.ingramcontent.com/pod-product-compliance
Lightning Source LLC
LaVergne TN
LVHW010358070526
838199LV00065B/5852